JUST say YES!

LEADER GUIDE

Other Abingdon Press Resources by Robert Schnase

Five Practices of Fruitful Living

Five Practices of Fruitful Congregations

Seven Levers: Missional Strategies for Conferences

Just Say Yes! Unleashing People for Ministry

Just Say Yes! Participant Guide

Just Say Yes! Devotional

Just Say Yes! DVD

Author of *Five Practices of Fruitful Congregations*

Robert Schnase
with Angela Olsen

JUST
say
YES!

UNLEASHING PEOPLE
FOR MINISTRY

LEADER GUIDE

Abingdon Press™

Nashville

JUST SAY YES! LEADER GUIDE:
UNLEASHING PEOPLE FOR MINISTRY
Copyright © 2016 by Abingdon Press

This book is printed on acid-free paper.

ISBN: 978-1-5018-2526-2

16 17 18 19 20 21 22 23 24 25—10 9 8 7 6 5 4 3 2 1
MANUFACTURED IN THE UNITED STATES OF AMERICA

Contents

Introduction

Y ou know the power of *Yes!* Saying *Yes* to Jesus Christ unleashes gifts and possibilities beyond measure. This *Yes* unlocks a life of boundless love on this earth and in eternity. This *Yes* opens eyes to see a world desperate for the grace we experience in Christ. It makes us long for a deeper relationship with God and compels us to grow in our love of neighbor. It empowers us with creativity and allows us to partner with God in kingdom building. The power of Christ propels us to make new disciples, serve the poor, and share God's love.

With all this passion and power propelling us, why do we find that the church is declining by so many measurements and in so many places? Why are we not making more disciples for the transformation of the world? Why are the ministries God placed on people's hearts being squashed before they even start? The book *Just Say Yes!* by Robert Schnase points to the reason. The default response in most churches is *No* rather than *Yes*. Many leaders and congregations struggle with stifling atmospheres of resistance. This church culture continually says *No* to new ideas and to people who are answering God's call to use their gifts and talents. Passionate and creative people are becoming so frustrated they leave the church. A different way of being and doing church is possible.

This *Just Say Yes!* study for leaders and congregants offers you tools to encourage a permission-giving culture in your church. Permission-giving churches recognize that all people have calls to ministry. These churches celebrate people's gifts, dreams, and passions and then encourage them in ministry. This is the difference between a *No* church and a Just Say Yes! church. Schnase says, "Vibrant, fruitful, growing congregations have been able to say *Yes* to things declining congregations say *No* to" (45). With the help of the Holy Spirit all churches can become permission-giving churches.

How to Use the Leader Guide

In *Just Say Yes!* Robert Schnase shows church leaders how to unleash people for fruitful ministry. He teaches leaders to spot their own naysaying and gives specific instructions for reversing the culture of *No* that has become so prevalent in many churches. Step by step, Schnase shows readers—pastors, other church leaders, and congregants—how to make significant change in their attitude and actions to become a permission-giving church.

This set of resources is the next step in the author's effort to reshape church leaders across the mainline denomination. *Just Say Yes! Leader Guide* gives church leaders what they need in order to begin implementing the principles in the original book. It starts with a group study experience for church leaders, facilitated by a senior leader (typically the pastor). The study can be done in as little as three hours or, if groups watch all the videos and do all the optional exercises and activities, up to six hours total. The sessions can be used as a single-day retreat or broken up into three to six separate sessions. They can be stand-alone sessions or incorporated into meetings for staff and lay leaders.

The leader guide includes instructions and guidance for leaders in planning, hosting, debriefing, and following up after the experience. Using this resource, plus the included customizable PowerPoint slides and the video stories of permission, a pastor or other key leader can effectively facilitate an extraordinary group experience resulting in transformation for the congregation.

The participant guide is a complete workbook for church leaders—staff and laity—who participate in the Just Say Yes! group experience. The study is designed for use with church councils, staff teams, committee chairs, ministry team leaders, and the like. The participant guide includes prompts to reinforce the material shared in the videos and by the facilitator, questions for reflection and discussion, and specific action steps for becoming permission-giving leaders in the church. It includes plenty of room for writing and note taking during the group experience. The group experience includes six inspiring and compelling videos from real church settings. Several additional video clips are also available for groups wanting to spend more time exploring ideas together.

For churches and leaders who want to go deeper, a four-week *Just Say Yes! Sermon and Worship Series* is available as a free download online. It includes sermon outlines, prayers, other liturgical texts for each week, and ideas for conducting the series. This series is a great way to bring the entire congregation on board after participants have first completed the small group study.

A printed four-week *Just Say Yes! Devotional* is also available. It can be used by individual church members autonomously or (ideally) used by every member as a personal study guide accompanying the four-week sermon and worship series. The material is flexible and accessible for all adult readers and can be done in one sitting or spread throughout the week.

Resources Available for Purchase as Part of Just Say Yes!

- The book *Just Say Yes!* by Robert Schnase
- The *Just Say Yes! Leader Guide* (this book)
  - instructions and script for the small group study leader
  - seven-segment devotional
  - suggestions for next steps
  - synopses of the *Just Say Yes!* videos
- The *Just Say Yes! Participant Guide*
  - instructions, content, and worksheets for the small group study
  - seven-segment devotional
- The *Just Say Yes! DVD*
  - all the video clips for the small group study plus additional videos for further discussion
  - an invitational video for promoting the study

The videos are also available for purchase and streaming individually at RobertSchnase.com and Cokesbury.com.

- The *Just Say Yes! Devotional*
  - stand-alone, personal study guide and devotional *and* a companion to the four-week *Just Say Yes! Sermon and Worship Series*

Free Resources Available Online at RobertSchnase.com and Cokesbury.com

- PowerPoint slides for the small group study presentations
- Customizable, printable promotional pieces for inviting leaders and congregants to the small group study and to the sermon and worship series

- Sermon outlines, liturgical helps, and other suggestions for a four-week
  Just Say Yes! Sermon and Worship Series. The weekly topics include:
    o Week 1—Say *Yes* to the Holy Spirit. (Everyone has gifts for
       ministry that are necessary for building the kingdom.)
    o Week 2—Say *Yes* to Your Calling. (God calls everyone to serve;
       explore where your gifts and passions meet the needs of your
       community.)
    o Week 3—Say *Yes* to Growing. (Foster spiritual growth and dis-
       cipleship; hone your understanding of God's purpose for your
       life.)
    o Week 4—Say *Yes* to Encouragement. (The work of the church
       is to encourage all people in their callings.)

Planning Tips

This study is designed to be flexible so that you can use the material however
it works best in your setting. You may do the study all at once as a three and a
half- to six-hour study. You might incorporate it as the focus of a church leaders' retreat. Perhaps in your context it will work best in smaller increments, such
as three one-hour sessions. Or you might use even smaller segments as a way to
begin staff or church council meetings, working through the material over a few
weeks or months.

The material is formatted in this leader guide (and in the participant guide) as
three sessions, but there are natural breaks in each session. So determine what will
work best for your participants, and divide the content according to your needs.

The instructions for facilitating the study are in italic type and brackets [ ].
The rest of the text is your "script"—suggested language for facilitating the ses-
sions. You will also note the extensive use of material from Robert Schnase's book.
Numbers within parentheses ( ) indicate page number references for *Just Say Yes!*

This study is organized into three sessions: Uncover the *Nos*, Unlock the
Power of *Yes*, and Unleash a Culture of *Yes*. These sessions move from personal
leadership development to cultivation of fruitfulness in the whole church. This
intentional movement from personal to church systems is rooted in the following
text in *Just Say Yes!*: "Congregations and operational systems never become more
permission-giving than the people who lead them. Leaders have a dispropor-
tionate influence on the culture and content of a church, and on the processes

that either restrain or multiply ministries" (93). This study experience will foster leadership development of pastors, church leaders, staff, and lay leaders. The aim is that your congregation will become a place of permission-giving where people are unleashed in fruitful ministry.

A Summary of the Sessions

Session 1—"Uncover the *Nos*" is designed to give examples of people and systems stifling creativity. It will offer challenges and time for self-discernment related to personal leadership roles in *No* situations.

Session 2—"Unlock the Power of *Yes*" connects us with the grace of God, which can overcome any negativity. After a time of prayer and Holy Communion, participants will spend time claiming their role as a permission-giving leader.

Session 3—"Unleash a Culture of *Yes*" fosters a time of team conversation and the creation of a permission-giving culture. This includes developing a framework to equip and encourage people to say *Yes* to God's call to serve using their gifts, talents, and passions.

After you complete the study material, the participants should journey individually through the seven-segment devotional. This will deepen their experience of the study and will increase the likelihood that the study has sustainable and lasting impact on those leaders and on your congregation.

Additionally, after the study is complete, consider the list of next steps found near the back of this book. These ideas will lead you to implementation and action based upon the participants' new understanding of the permission-giving church. Next steps will help you put the rubber to the road.

Finally, consider doing the four-week *Just Say Yes! Sermon and Worship Series* after you've completed this study. The study will change your church's leadership, but the sermon and worship series could change your entire congregation.

How to Facilitate the Study

Your role as leader is important. Read *Just Say Yes!* and read through this leader script multiple times to make it your own. Watch all of the videos, either on the DVD or (available for purchase) streamed online. Make notes about the video stories and the ways they resonate for your context. You may find that some of the optional videos will be quite powerful for the participants.

You will need to keep the conversation moving and be aware of time. First you must decide how long each session will be. Review the material and, if you are breaking it up into shorter segments, determine how to break up the sessions according to the time you have available. You'll find recommended time frames for each component of the sessions; use these as your guide. A word of caution: This material may challenge you and your participants. In fact, it should! Together you will expose some negative scenarios in your church and will learn how to transform them to a hopeful *Yes* culture. Be prepared to redirect the conversation if negativity rises up, and do not be afraid to pause for prayer. Keeping the conversation centered on Christ and underlying everything with grace will profoundly enhance the experience.

Recommendations for Preparation Prior to Training

- Pray.

- Read *Just Say Yes: Unleashing People for Ministry*.

- Read this *Just Say Yes! Leader Guide* carefully. There is a lot of text, so get familiar with the material so it flows easily and you can make appropriate adjustments for your ministry setting.

- Order books and participant guides for each participant. This training assumes each participant has read the *Just Say Yes!* book prior to the study.

- Set date and place for retreat or study.

- Watch the videos. Determine if you will watch any of the optional videos with your group.

- Add your own questions or activities, if you like, to make the study more personalized for your context and for your participants.

- Consider the space where you'll be leading the sessions. Plan ways to enhance the environment, if necessary.

- Determine where you will take breaks during the sessions, if necessary.

- Personally distribute books along with the invitation postcard. We recommend handing this out six weeks prior to the training to give people a week to read each chapter.

- Invite participants to bring a Bible and their copy of Robert Schnase's book *Just Say Yes!*

- Invite volunteers to help you with set-up and tear-down for each session.

- Invite volunteers as needed for each session. For instance, you will need people to serve communion during session 2. Ideally, your volunteers will be people who are not participating in the training so that participants can fully focus on the study experience.

- Keep praying and fast (if approved by your physician).

This is a list of suggested supplies:

- computer with PowerPoint

- projector with screen

- pens

- chalkboard or dry erase board

- music for Holy Communion in session 2 (live music, a CD, or YouTube versions of the music—songs suggestions are listed in session 2)

- room or altar decorations to enhance the atmosphere of the training (Christ candle; locks and keys; block letters spelling *Yes*; red, teal and navy cloths—get creative)

- blank paper for confession experience in session 2 ("letting go")

- baskets or containers for confessions in session 2 ("letting go")

- communion supplies (gluten free, if needed)

- snacks, drinks, and lunch (if appropriate for time of training or retreat)

- anointing oil

Following the training, please encourage participants and your church to continue growing as permission-giving leaders and as a permission-giving culture. Encourage participants to do the seven-segment devotional, and consider ways to hold one another accountable for that. Also consider ways to use the next steps section at the end of the guide to facilitate implementation and action based on what you've learned through the study. Finally, set a time to do the four-week *Just Say Yes! Sermon and Worship Series* in your congregation. If you are not the pastor, share the planning resources for this series (available online) with your pastor. If possible, purchase copies of the four-week *Just Say Yes! Devotional* for each member of your congregation, or make these inexpensive books available for them to purchase.

You have taken a bold and courageous step in leading this training experience. Congratulations! Through this process, may God unleash a creative and passionate chorus of Christ-centered *Yeses* in your church and beyond!

Faith is the reality of what we hope for, the proof of what we don't see.

—Hebrews 11:1

Instructions and Script for the Group Study Sessions

Uncover the *Nos*

Prepare for This Session

- Arrange the tables and chairs so participants can comfortably see the video screen and have discussions with two or three others.

- Create an altar space to enhance the spiritual experience of the training. Ideas for the altar include a cross, a candle, cloths in the color scheme of the book (red, tan, teal, and navy), communion set, large letters spelling out *Yes!*

- Participants will need a participant guide and a pen; if you are responsible for distributing these, set them out at each participant's place.

- Have a chalkboard or dry erase board ready. Write the faulty assumptions ("This Is OUR Church," "The Center," and "It's All about Me") in three columns to use in the group exercise.

[10 minutes]

Thank you for coming to this leader study [or retreat] and for taking the time to read *Just Say Yes! Unleashing People for Ministry* by Robert Schnase. It is written for people like you whose passion has been simmering for years, who yearn to be told *Yes!* and be part of a *Yes!* church culture. This kind of culture takes intentionality. The book illustrates how people, pastors, and churches say *"No* in a thousand ways to new ideas, ministry initiatives, and creative people" (ix). Perhaps these examples resonate with your own experience of leadership and church. Have you experienced a time when you really believed God was calling you to champion a new ministry? You believed you could make a difference, but people started telling you all the reasons why your ideas wouldn't work. You started hearing all the *Nos*. Instead of listening for possibilities and collaborating with you to find ways to overcome barriers, other people shut you down.

Jesus Christ invites us to be encouragers and that is why this study is so important. The world is broken, hurting, and in need of hope. As people who have said the ultimate *Yes* to Jesus, we are called to share the love, healing, and eternal hope we have through Jesus Christ. Yet, we continually hear the statistics on church decline. People talk about how "we've always done it that way" or how you can never get anything done in church, often in a joking manner. But it is no joke when our tendency toward *No* blocks the work of Christ. Sometimes we do not even realize how often we, the people around us, our systems, and even our buildings say *No*. Sometimes we as leaders are part of saying *No* to people's heart-felt passion to serve and grow closer to God. At the center of this study is a desire for people to draw closer to God and neighbor, to make active disciples of Jesus Christ, and to live out the mission to which Christ calls us. But we can't live out that mission, as people or as the church, if we default to a *No* anytime new ideas are offered.

You are here today to learn tools to move your personal leadership and our church's culture from postures of *No* to *Yes*. Together, we will uncover the *Nos* in our church leadership (people and systems), unlock the power of *Yes* in ourselves, and unleash a culture of *Yes* here at [*insert your church's name*].

This work of personal reflection, study, and team development is crucial, and we cannot do it alone. Jesus said to the disciples long ago and says to us today, "If you love me, you will keep my commandments. I will ask the Father, and he will send another Companion, who will be with you forever.... The Companion, the Holy Spirit, whom the Father will send in my name, will teach you everything and will remind you of everything I told you" (John 14:15-16, 26).

Therefore, together, let us seek the guidance offered. Through prayer we will be reminded we have the power of God propelling us forward.

Prayer

I invite you now to find a posture that helps you open to God—perhaps open or lifted hands. This prayer will be said in unison. The words are in your participant guide (and on the screen). Please pray with me.

> [*Say in unison*] Faithful and life-giving God, please create in this room a sacred space filled with your Holy Spirit. We come here to learn more about you and

your call to lead in this church. Open our hearts and minds to the work we must do to honor you. Reveal to us the stifling impact *Nos* have on the gifts, talents, creativity, and passion of your people. Help us feel your grace in moments of conviction and then offer grace to each other through this work. Give us courage to follow you from *No* to *Yes*. By the end of our time together, help us each to say boldly *Yes* Lord, *Yes!* It is in the name of our Savior, Jesus Christ, we pray. Amen.

Introductions

We are going to take a few minutes to make sure everyone knows each other. Let's go around the room saying your name and why you said *Yes* to being here today.

Let's take few minutes to hear Bishop Robert Schnase give his reasons for writing the book. This video also introduces two permission-giving leaders: Rev. Jennifer Weekes-Klein and Rev. Jim Downing, whom we will hear more from in sessions 2 and 3.

Video: "Just Say Yes! Introductory Video"

[5 minutes]

Bishop Robert Schnase shares how *Just Say Yes! Unleashing People for Ministry* can offer hope for those people whose passion has been simmering for years.

Stories of *No*

[10 minutes, including group sharing]

In *Just Say Yes!* we see how people yearn to be set free for ministry, yet so many parts of church life say *No* to ministry. Our aim here is to unleash people for the ministry of Jesus Christ. To do this, even though it is challenging, we need to explore the reality of *No* in church life. I am going to share a few *No* stories. Before I do, please know the purpose of sharing these stories is not to hurt people but to see the obstacles for our future ministry so that together we can work to remove them. Grace and forgiveness is key as we do this work today.

Session 1

[Below are stories of No *that were not included in the book. Please share several stories. You can use the ones offered here, your own personal stories from your life or ministry, or retell a story from the book. This will expose how a culture of* No *can be destructive for ministry. A word of caution: Sharing stories from your current setting may be hurtful. It may be best to use the stories from* Just Say Yes! *or your own life here so that participants don't feel as if they or their ministries are being publicly called out. Trust that the Holy Spirit will reveal the obstacles present in your church's culture and will empower you and your leaders to remove them. As you begin this study, be sure to lay a groundwork of grace and hope.]*

VBS Story—A church decided they only had space for thirty children at their Vacation Bible School. For this reason, they would not allow sign-ups from the community unless all congregation members were signed up first. Instead of looking outward to make new disciples, they said *No* to their neighbors.

Children's Wing—A group within a church decided to donate money for a new children's wing as long as they could also meet there once a week. They chose fancy carpet and furniture. At the dedication for the new wing, there was no evidence of children using the space. The space was pristine with no children's murals or toys, and it even included signs like "no drinks." Instead of focusing on encouraging a new generation of believers, they said *No* to children.

Signs—A church was located in an ethnically diverse community. They wanted to be a multigenerational and multiethnic church. They built a new and wonderful playground for the community. Yet there were signs of "Welcome" in English and signs of "No Entry" written in Spanish. Instead of saying all are invited and welcome, they said *No* to diversity.

New Members—A new member came to the pastor and church council with an idea to help people reenter society after prison. This would include teaching cooking classes in the kitchen, using the library computers for resume building, and organizing budgeting classes. The first committee said you have to have it approved by the trustees, then the finance committee, then the...you name it committee. Ultimately the obstacles overcame the new member's passion; he gave up and ultimately left the church. Instead of offering encouragement, reconciliation, and grace, they said *No* to passion, hospitality, and hope.

Group Sharing

In addition to these stories of *No*, were there any that really struck you from the book? Take a moment to imagine what these *No* scenarios do to the life of a congregation. How do you feel when you are told *No*?

Checklist of *Nos*

[15 minutes, including group discussion]

Just Say Yes! outlines thirteen ways people say *No*. Our challenge is to recognize the *Nos* in our midst. In your session 1 participant workbook you will find a checklist of *Nos*. Take a few moments to check all the types of *Nos* you have received personally as well as all the types of *Nos* you have said yourself. If you want more details about the *Nos* listed, please feel free to reread pages 3–8 in *Just Say Yes!* [*Offer the participants time to read through and place a check in each box that applies to them.*]

- You're Not the Pastor—Leadership and authority should only come through the pastor.

- I Don't Need That, So Why Should We Do It?—This ministry does not benefit me, so it is not important.

- Only Five People Signed Up—The effort this will take is not worth it for so few people.

- They're Not Our Members Anyway—Guests are not as valuable as members.

- That's Our Room—Your ministry is not as important as what *we* do in this room.

- That Will Never Work Here (and I'll See That It Doesn't!)—I don't see this working, so I will sabotage the ministry.

- They Can Just Join Us—New people do not need new ministries, they need to fit into our mold (existing groups and ministries).

- Analysis Paralysis—We need to think this through in such detail that nothing will happen.

7

- You're Too Young, Too New, or Too Different—You do not look the same as me so you are not welcome and your ideas do not matter.

- You're Doing It All Wrong—You are not doing it my way, so do not do it.

- You Didn't Ask Me First—Without my permission this cannot happen.

- Don't Rock the Boat—You are changing things and I don't like it.

- Things Won't Be the Same—Change is scary and hard, so do not try anything new.

- Others (fill in the blank with your own category)_____

Group Sharing

After you complete your checklists, please break up into groups of two to three. Here are your two topics for discussion: (1) Describe one of the times you were on the receiving end of a *No* response—what happened to your ministry idea? (2) Have you ever been the one saying *No?*—what happened to that ministry idea?

[*Bring the group back together after 10 minutes or sooner if conversation slows.*]

Optional Break

[*If you are using this material in more than three sessions (for example, as a learning time at the beginning of council or team meetings), this is a suggested break point. Here is helpful language to use to begin this shortened section.*]

Last time we met, we explored the thirteen ways people say *No* in the life of the church according to *Just Say Yes!* by Robert Schnase. Uncovering the *No* experiences in our church is crucial to moving forward and unleashing our church for ministry. This meeting, we will take some time to explore some reasons why we say *No*.

Faulty Assumptions Leading to *No*

[10 minutes; use pages 8–10 in *Just Say Yes!*]

We have named and discussed some *No* situations in the life of our church. It is curious to me that there are so many since most of us wake up in the morning with good intentions to say *Yes* to the work of Jesus Christ in the world. Yet in the course of our lives we say *No*, knowingly and unknowingly, to the movement of God's spirit. Why? Schnase says, "Many reasons why people say *No* derive from faulty assumptions" (8). *Just Say Yes!* describes three faulty assumptions. To refresh your memory, I will offer a simple reminder of the concepts.

This Is Our Church

Instead of being centered on Christ, we forget we are Christ's body. "When we act as if the church belongs to us—the pastor, the staff, the leaders, the members—then the criteria for why we say *Yes* or *No* becomes what *we* prefer, what *we* want, what *we* seek" (8).

Ideas Come from the Center

Instead of allowing people to discover unmet needs in the community and encouraging them to develop a ministry, church systems and people say, *No the ideas have to come from core leadership in the church.* "The assumption that ideas must begin at the center and be controlled from the center fosters a tendency to say *No* to new ideas that come from anywhere else" (10).

It's All about Us

Instead of asking "What is God calling us to do?" we more often ask "What's in it for me?" We also ask, "'What will I have to do? What will it cost me?' This natural and understandable response limits mission, stifles creativity, and squelches the genuine call of God" (10).

Group Exercise

[10 minutes]

[*Have a dry erase board, chalkboard, or large paper. Before the session, make three columns with "This Is OUR Church," ideas from "The Center," and "It's All about Me" at the top of the columns.*]

We are going to explore these faulty assumptions and how they negatively impact our ministry for Jesus Christ. I need a volunteer to write on the board.

Shout out the word or words that come to mind when you hear the following three questions and our volunteer will write down the thoughts.

9

- What happens when we say "This is OUR church"?

- What happens when we believe ideas only come from our core leadership team, "the center"?

- What happens when we say "it's all about me"?

Now I need three people to read scriptures.
First, we will hear the greatest commandment in Matthew 22:34-40.
Now, the great compassion in Matthew 25:34-39.
Finally, the great commission in Matthew 28:19-20.
In light of Jesus's words, what words need to be replaced on the board?
How do these words from our savior change the assumptions?
Before we take a break, please write down one of the *No* scenarios you have experienced, either said or received. These scenarios will be used in the subsequent sessions, so this step is important!

Break

[10 minutes]

Session 2

Unlock the Power of Yes

- Prepare bread and juice (or wine) for Holy Communion. If you are in the United Methodist tradition and not a pastor, you will want to have a pastor consecrate the elements prior to or during the study.

- Have music ready to play during Holy Communion if you choose to enhance the experience with music. If the music will be played live, discuss the selections, timing, and any other details with the musicians.

- Place a blank piece of paper at each seat.

- Have a basket ready for the Letting Go experience.

In session 1, we uncovered some of the *No* scenarios in our church ministries. These can stifle creativity and people's willingness to answer God's call on their lives. It is possible to change a negative culture into one of positivity and hope. This is our job as leaders!

[70 minutes]

In this session we will spend some time in self-reflection about our role as leaders. We will do the important work of confessing our shortcomings to God and will actively receive the grace offered through Holy Communion. After this experience of grace, we will move into an exploration of what permission-giving leadership really looks like. A significant part of leadership is about the tone we set when we encounter obstacles to ministry. Watch this video example.

11

Video: "A New Way of Being: Sturgeon UMC"

[5 minutes]

The story of Sturgeon United Methodist Church was all too common: too small, too old, too tired. Under the unifying direction of Rev. Mike Will, they joined forces with the four other local churches and forged a new way of being church to their broader community.

When Rev. Mike Will presented the idea for a new ministry to his congregation, the response was not surprising. They said, we are only fifteen people and cannot possibly take on a dream this big. Yet with the hopeful and encouraging leadership of Rev. Will, they joined forces with the four other local churches and forged a new way of being church to their broader community. By taking a risk and learning together they said *Yes* to God. Now their church no longer remains silent and closed, but helps serve 280 families (almost 950 people) at a free food pantry and 350 people monthly at a thrift store. Lives are being blessed and a church is growing in the grace of God.

Intentional Leadership Reflection

[10 minutes]

Just like Rev. Mike Will, we all face challenges in church leadership. Leaders who say *Yes* to God must understand who they are as leaders. If Rev. Will had started listing all the reasons not to do this new ministry, the people of Sturgeon United Methodist Church would have said *No*. They would have claimed human possibilities, not God possibilities. Thankfully they said *Yes* to God even with all the challenges.

As leaders, do we bring negativity or hope?

Do we bring fear or joy?

Are we staying connected with the one who called us into leadership?

In *Just Say Yes!*, Schnase shares a revelation about his leadership after a purposeful time of "rest, renewal, and learning" (93). After a twelve-week sabbatical, he returned to work and noticed some new ministries in place. Schnase writes,

12

"As I looked at the fall program, I thought, 'these are great ideas. Why didn't we think of these things when I was there?' Then it dawned on me: maybe we didn't initiate these things before now *because* I had been there!" (93).

He reveals that "sometimes leaders are the obstacles to innovation without knowing it" (94). How can we discern if we are knowingly and unknowingly creating barriers to ministry?

> If you want to explore failure-tolerant leadership more deeply with your group, reread pages 104–6 in *Just Say Yes!* and watch the extra video titled "Failure-Tolerant Leadership."
>
> Rev. Tina Harris, pastor of Grand Avenue Temple in Kansas City, reminds leaders how, sometimes, failures can be the best example of following Jesus.

As I offer you some ways to evaluate your role as leader, please write down your answers and thoughts in the workbook as we walk through this process together. Here are some ways to start your reflection:

1. Ask yourself, "Am I ever a stumbling block to others or the ministry of Jesus Christ in the world?"

   This is a very general question, so think back specifically to the *No* scenario you wrote down in session 1. In light of this question, what role did you play in the *No*? If you were the recipient of the *No*, when was a different time looking back you played a part in stifling a ministry or project? [*Give the participants a moment or two to write their own answers.*]

2. When faced with a leadership decision are you conscious of the internal struggle Schnase illustrated in the book?

   Schnase said, "when I'm asked whether I think we should go forward with an idea, if I don't monitor myself to focus on the larger mission, my default response reflects my personal preference and my perception of the impact that the decision will have on me" (10).

3. Jesus said it another way: "[Jesus] turned and said to Peter, 'Get behind me, Satan. You are a stone that could make me stumble, for you are not thinking God's thoughts but human thoughts'" (Matt 16:23).

   Peter needed to take a step back, recognize his errors, and remember to follow Jesus's lead again.

Could Jesus be saying the same things to us when we set our mind on human things like control and selfishness?

When you are part of decision making at church, what guides you? [*Give the participants a minute or two to write down their answers.*]

4. Thankfully, even though our leadership has not been perfect, Jesus calls us to lead anyway. Not long after Jesus reprimands Peter, Peter is asked to experience the Transfiguration. Peter sees Jesus glorified and is told: "Get up.... Don't be afraid" (Matt 17:7). What an extraordinary blessing from God. No matter our past failings, Jesus invites us into amazing opportunities for ministry through his forgiving grace. Jesus is a failure-tolerant leader.

We are going to take some time now to grab onto that freely offered grace.

Unlocking the Power of Yes through the Forgiving Grace of Jesus Christ

[15 minutes, including the video]

The grace of God is going to help us overcome the obstacles preventing us from being truly permission-giving leaders and help us fully say *Yes* to following Jesus. In this next video, Rev. Jennifer Weekes-Klein will offer suggestions on spiritual practices that can move us from *No* to *Yes* through Jesus Christ.

Video: "Unlocking the Power of Yes: Becoming More Permission Giving"

[3 minutes]

Rev. Jennifer Weekes-Klein, senior pastor of Country Club United Methodist Church in Kansas City, shares the necessary personal, spiritual work that needs to be done in order to unlock the power of Yes in your life.

Rev. Weekes-Klein says a key to unlocking ourselves for ministry is letting go of negativity, our need for control, and fear of change. Shifting from *No* to *Yes* requires openness to the transformative power of Jesus. This is a movement from personal control to trust in God. As Rev. Weekes-Klein and Schnase suggest, we must take time away to open ourselves to God's voice. That's what we will do now. Together we are going to take some time to humbly seek God in prayer. Our hope is this time will foster a spirit of openness so we can all fully receive the love and grace of God through communion.

[*Give silence and space for people to complete this exercise.*] On the blank piece of paper in front of you, take a few moments to write down the *Nos* you want God to transform into *Yeses.*

Take the time you need to really communicate with God. You can make it in the form of a prayer, a list of all the ways you want God to help you lead with trust and hope, a poem, or a drawing of *Nos.*

The checklist of *Nos* from the session 1 worksheet and the following list are here to help you get started. These lists can help you recognize any negativity you may bring to ministry and want to give away to reach your full potential in God.

List of Negative Attitudes and Actions That Stifle Ministry

(Use this along with the session 1 checklist of *Nos.*)

- Fear—Fear of the unknown or change stops me from trying anything new.

- Passive aggressive behavior—Disparaging or snide remarks, sabotaging others, and so on.

- Negative attitude or thinking—Church is too old, too small, too poor, too _____.

- Unwillingness to help others—It will cost me too much; it is too hard; it is not my passion; or it's not for me.

- Harsh correction of others—That is not how I think it should be done; that is not how "we" do it.

15

- Body language—Disapproving glances, shaking of the head, crossing of the arms.

- Grudges—Holding on to past hurts, we sometimes let those color our decision and hurt others.

[*After participants are finished writing, invite them to prepare for confession.*]

Once you have written down your confession or plea for God's help, crumple it up and hold it tightly in your fist. Please join me in this prayer of confession. The words of the prayer are printed in your participant guide (and on the screen). It is in leader-response form, so I will read the *L* line and then you will join in the bold *P* responses.

Prayer of Confession

L: Lord, we confess our day-to-day failure to fully say *Yes* to You.

P: Lord, we confess to you.

L: Lord, we confess we often fail to love with all we have and are, often because we do not fully understand what loving means, often because we are afraid of risking ourselves.

P: Lord, we confess to you.

L: Lord, we confess we sometimes forget this church is yours.

P: We sometimes center our ministry on personal preferences and desires.

L: Lord, we confess that by silence and ill-considered words

P: we have built stumbling blocks to the creativity and passions of your people.

L: Lord, we confess that by selfishness and lack of sympathy

P: we have stifled generosity and missed opportunities to serve the least of these.

All: Holy Spirit, speak to us. Help us listen to your word of forgiveness so we might lessen our tight-fisted hold on leadership. Right now, help us open our hands to receive your grace. Allow us to become leaders of hope, innovation, and grace. Come, fill this moment and free us from sin. Amen.

(Adapted from #893 in *The United Methodist Hymnal*)

Holy Communion

[20 minutes with 5 minutes of silence following communion]

[*This celebration of Holy Communion is written in a United Methodist format, but we invite you to adjust the service in light of your church's doctrine, traditions, and practices. In The United Methodist Church, we believe communion is an open table, and in this setting we encourage you to serve by intinction (dip the piece of bread into a chalice of juice). We recommend using "A Service of Word and Table I" in* The United Methodist Hymnal *or use the specialized Great Thanksgiving communion service offered over the next few pages. Participants will be invited to bring their note of confession to leave at the altar. Please provide a basket or some way for the notes to be held with a sense of privacy. Participants will then be invited to receive the bread and juice with open hands. It will be meaningful for the servers to hand the bread to recipients. Here are some song suggestions to play during the serving of communion that are available on YouTube: "Yes" by Shekinah Glory Ministry, "We Are Yours" by I Am They, "One Bread, One Body" #620 in* The United Methodist Hymnal, *"The Table" by Chris Tomlin.*]

We are here to acknowledge our need for God and our desire to be leaders of encouragement and hope. We are invited to the table of our Lord Jesus Christ. This experience is a means of grace and its power is infinite to transform lives.

Optional Liturgy of Great Thanksgiving

On the night when Jesus gave himself for us, he lovingly met with his disciples. He called each of them to learn from him and follow him. He saw in them gifts crucial to share the good news he had to offer the world. In his last, living moments with them he took time to teach them how to stay connected with him always. In those moments, he offered them forgiveness, love, and an everlasting promise of relationship. He took the bread, thanked God, and broke the bread. [*Break the bread.*] He taught them the miraculous power of how his broken body can heal them. Then he took the cup and made it more than wine. He told them it was his blood poured out for the forgiveness of sins.

Jesus invites you to hear today; he is calling you to learn from him and follow him. He has given you each gifts and talents crucial for ministry as part of the body of Christ. He invites you to renew your commitment to follow him. He invites you to remember his never-ending love through this bread and juice. He

17

speaks words of forgiveness and grace into your hearts and minds. He has done everything necessary to help you be unafraid and expectant about God's work in your midst. Please open yourself up to God as I pray.

Prayer

Dear Lord, you have heard our confessions. Help us truly let go of any negativity blocking your powerful Spirit's movement and whole-heartedly receive your forgiveness with open hands. We hear you forgive us. Pour out your Holy Spirit upon on us and on these gifts. Make this bread and juice be your body and blood, so we will be forever connected with you and the rest of your body redeemed by your blood. Give us all we need to forgive others, to grab onto your grace and to be the leaders you call us to be. Help us to be unafraid of saying *Yes* to you and all you ask of us. Invigorate us now with this incredibly, selfless gift of love. May it inspire a community of people who say *Yes* to you. In the saving power of Jesus Christ. Amen.

You are invited now to unclench your fist and leave your confessions at the table of the Lord. Please come with open hands and hearts to receive this awe-inspiring gift of forgiveness and love. After you receive, please feel free to stay in prayer as long as you need. We will have a time of silence after receiving communion to allow us all to process the impact of God's freely given grace on our lives. [*Play music as the participants receive communion and allow a good five minutes of silence following the last person receiving.*]

Silence

[5 minutes following communion]

[*The following text is found in the participant guide, so please direct participants to answer the question during the silence.*]

During this time of silence, take a moment to fill in the answer to the following question at the bottom of your session 2 worksheet.

Have you begun letting go of the hurts or guilt about the *No* scenario you wrote down at the bottom of the session 1 worksheet?

If not, keep the worksheet as a reminder to continue the process of letting go. The devotion guide we will introduce next will help you on your journey.

A Time of Self-Reflection

Optional Break

[*If you are using this material in more than three sessions (for example, as a learning time at the beginning of council or team meetings), this is a suggested break point. Here is helpful language to use to begin this shortened section.*]

When we last met, our time was spent reflecting on anything holding us back from fully saying *Yes* to the movement of God's spirit in this place. We intentionally sought the grace of God through confession, prayer, and communion. This grace continues to unlock our ability to be permission-giving leaders.

Permission-Giving Leadership

[10 minutes]

In light of the forgiveness, love, hope and grace that Holy Communion has unlocked in us, we have work to do. We can begin the journey toward becoming permission-giving leaders. Your role is crucial. *Just Say Yes!* illuminates how "congregations and operational systems never become more permission-giving than the people who lead them" (93). "In a culture of *Yes*, leaders are purveyors of hope. They believe in new life, new birth, and resurrection. They believe that God is at work in the minds and hearts of people...for ministries they never imagined" (95).

The book gives some example characteristics of permission-giving leaders. Here is a summary of those characteristics found on pages 95–99:

- They trust people and that God is at work in people and processes.
- They are responsible risk-takers.
- They grow their churches by multiplication and not just by addition.
- They know how to listen and get out of the way by opening options rather than closing them.
- They hold high expectations, are clear about the mission, and are confident about the future.

19

- They seldom say *No* but ask encouraging questions to help discernment.

- They know exercising too much control limits creativity and capacity of staff and volunteers.

- They give space for people to answer their calling and value the initiatives of all people.

- They never go it alone.

- They have the ability to say *Yes* even to people who think differently from them.

- They develop habits that keep them freshly engaged with young people, new people, visitors, and those who do not yet belong to the church.

On this list, which characteristics are the most exciting and the most challenging to you? Write down the ones you want to make a priority in your ministry. Keep these to help you develop your leadership in coming weeks. [*Give participants a few minutes to read through this list and write down their priorities in their participant guides.*]

Becoming a permission-giving leader is not an instantaneous transition. For this reason, you will find a seven-segment devotional at the back of your participant guide. You are invited to invest more time after this small group study to deepen the experience, to make permission-giving a sustainable, strong, ongoing characteristic in your life and in our congregation. The devotion contains both practical and spiritual disciplines to help us each develop into a permission-giving leader. This time of devotion will help you keep the priorities you just wrote down for growing in your leadership.

Guided Autonomy

[10-15 minutes, including the video and group work]

A significant part of being a permission-giving leader comes from the concept of guided autonomy (70). There is a fine line between leaders who abandon their people and those who micromanage ministries. This balance happens when leaders guide and hold people accountable to the mission and vision of the church and support people to initiate and champion new ministries. Check out this powerful video example of guided autonomy.

Video: "Hope in the Baking: Bridge Bread"

[8 minutes]

Lafayette Park United Methodist Church is an urban local church in one of the oldest parts of St. Louis. Through prayer and discernment, a small group of disciples began exploring the ministry and business of social enterprise and Bridge Bread was born.

In St. Louis, Missouri, Lafayette Park United Methodist Church is a powerful example of a permission-giving culture. Bridge Bread is a social enterprise ministry for the homeless. In order for this extraordinary ministry to begin a number of things had to occur: a man named Fred had to believe God was speaking to him, he had to discover a permission-giving leader in Rev. Kathleen Wilder, and he had to have a permission-giving culture at his home congregation of Lafayette Park UMC.

Something remarkable happened when all those elements were present. Rev. Wilder led a Bible study on ethics and poverty. Church members like Fred attended and were inspired. Then Rev. Wilder went on vacation but made sure her people had a place to continue to meet and dream in her absence. Upon her return, Bridge Bread and other ministries were born and already in the works to bless others. In the video, she says to pastor (and leaders), "Give yourself a break. Don't make yourself have to know it all—you never know it all. You were never intended to know it all. This is why we are part of a Christian community." Leaders are called to equip, encourage, and unleash. That does not mean we have to do everything or know everything.

Group Discussion and Accountability

When you think about the type of leader you are, do you tend toward the controlling, micromanaging, need-to-know-it-all side or are you closer to the leave-people-alone, abandon-and-never-follow-through side?

What is one thing you can do to find that balance point and lead with guided autonomy?

Name it, write it down, and then ask others here to gracefully hold you accountable to this goal.

Keep these goals in mind along with the priorities for growing as a permission-giving leader, and work on them during your devotion time following this training.

Break

[10 minutes. *Use this break time to recruit three people to act out the role-play exercise during session 3. The role-play script is found in session 3 of the participant guide.*]

Session 3

Unleash a Culture of Yes

Prepare for This Session

- Invite three people to act out the role-play script found in the participant guide.

- Write your church's mission and vision statement on the board for use in the permission-giving culture development section.

- Have a vial (or more) of anointing oil to be prepared for the close of this session.

- This session is intended to help participants see the joy and creativity of permission-giving churches. Facilitate a creative atmosphere by having soft, upbeat Christian music playing when participants enter. Offer snacks, have dry erase boards or other places for small groups to write and work together—or anything else you can think of to enhance inspiration.

[60 minutes]

In the last session, we worked to unlock the power of *Yes*. Our goal was to connect with the grace of God through prayer and Holy Communion. This grace can overcome any negativity and help us claim our roles as permission-giving leaders.

This session, we will move from an emphasis on our personal leadership to the development of permission-giving systems in this church.

Core of the Book

[15 minutes, including video and discussion]

According to Robert Schnase, the core of the *Just Say Yes!* book is "vibrant,

23

fruitful, growing congregations have been willing to say *Yes* to things that declining congregations have said *No* to" (45). He also says,

> Missional churches shift a *No* culture to a culture that helps people cultivate their calling and creativity. People need to be unleashed for ministry—encouraged and emboldened, equipped and sent out. Unleashed means to set free, to unbind from restraint, to set loose.... *Unleashed* also means to "set forcefully in motion."...When we set people free to do the work of God, the spirit of Christ propels us into places and into ministries we could never have imagined. (x)

An unleashed church is an exciting place to be where more and more people know the love and grace of Jesus Christ.

Unleashing Systems: Creating a Culture Shift

It is simple to say we will shift from a *No* culture to an unleashed *Yes* culture, but how? We are about to watch a video of a congregation that made the switch. Over time, Rev. Jim Downing has been able to lay a foundation changing the default from *No* to *Yes* and now serves a culture unleashing people for ministry. This foundation is built by continually pointing to the hope we have in Jesus Christ.

Video: "Unleashing Systems: Creating a Culture Shift"
[5 minutes]

Rev. Jim Downing, senior pastor of First United Methodist Church of Sedalia, shares how leaders can work to create a cultural shift from a *No* culture to a permission-giving culture.

Group Activity

[*Use the board to accumulate a list of qualities in those leaders. Give the participants ten minutes to discuss these questions.*]

Rev. Downing talks about three types of people: complainers, critics, and champions. Name some champions you have met.

What about them unleashes others?

What would shutting down the complaints department mean in our church, and how could we make that happen?

Permission-Giving Culture Development

[35 minutes, including video, role-play, and question development]

Churches that creatively say *Yes*, like Rev. Downing's church, encourage dreaming.

Just Say Yes! says, "Instead of the church council adopting a program and then convincing volunteers to implement it, a ministry begins with the sense of calling and enthusiasm among people at the margins, builds momentum, and then becomes recognized and adopted by the council" (9).

How do we make this happen here?

With the help of three volunteers, we are going to act out a few possible scenarios for how church can function.

Role-Playing Exercise

[*Have the three people you recruited during the break act out the script. The script is printed in the participant guide. This exercise will help participants see a No response and then what is possible when they develop a permission-giving culture.*]

Optional Break

[*If you are using this material in more than three sessions (for example, as a learning time at the beginning of council or team meetings), this is a suggested break point. Here is helpful language to use to begin this shortened section.*]

During our last time together, we started to unleash a *Yes* culture here in our church. Remember we discussed how we need champions not complainers, and we ended with a role-play exercise. Scenario 1 explored a *No* response and then scenario 2 showed what is possible when we develop a permission-giving culture.

Framework Development

To make sure scenario 1 does not happen in our congregation, we, as a team, need a framework for making decisions. We are going to do everything we can to make this a church of people unleashed for ministry in the name of Jesus Christ. Using all the insights we have gained so far we will create a structure to equip, strengthen, and unleash them to ministry. We must acknowledge that sometimes *No* is the right answer (87), but even better is having a framework to encourage people in their dreams. In this next video, Rev. Matt Miofsky will describe this scenario.

To explore more fully when *No* is the right answer, reread, "Sometimes *No* Is the Right Answer" in *Just Say Yes!* on pages 87–90.

Video: "Permission-Giving Leadership: When *No* Is the Right Answer"

[3 minutes]

Rev. Matt Miofsky, senior pastor of The Gathering in St. Louis, stresses that ideas that do not align with mission, priorities, and the spirit of the church are legitimate reasons to say *No*.

Even in a *Yes*-oriented culture, one has to protect values, quality, framework, and purpose. *No* is still important. Rev. Matt Miofsky emphasizes that sticking to the particular vision for a community in a particular time and place allows the community to remain vibrant and healthy. Rev. Miofsky reminds us that shutting down people who are enthusiastic is counter to our calling.

The key question to keep in mind as we move forward is, "How can we say *Yes* to an element of people's ideas even when our initial, internal reaction is *No*?"

So now we will develop our permission-giving system. To develop our framework for decision-making, Schnase gives some launching points. All of these are listed in your participant guide. He offers missional assumptions to counter the faulty ones we discussed in session 1. He also gives missional question examples from two permission-giving congregations. You will notice the questions for each of the congregations are different. They represent specific congregations and their role in the body of Christ. The questions we develop will be specific to our setting. As a team, let us take some time to discern our questions. **Please**

remember, this is not a time for brainstorming ministry ideas. This is the time to set a framework for encouraging the people in our midst to share their ideas and dreams for using the gifts and talents God has given them!

[*Just Say Yes! emphasizes the importance of adopting the missional assumptions as a foundation for this process. To start the conversation, it will be beneficial to walk through the missional assumptions and compare them to your own mission and vision statements.*]

Let us begin with the *Just Say Yes!* missional assumptions.

Robert Schnase's Missional Assumptions

1. Everyone has gifts for ministry.

2. God calls everyone to service and ministry.

3. The ministries of the church should foster spiritual growth and discipleship.

4. The church's mission is outward-focused.

5. The work of the church is to encourage people in their callings. (55–62)

Group Discussion

How do we live out these assumptions well in this church? Which of the assumptions do we need to work on adopting here? Why do these need to be foundational to our ministry? [*Use this time to establish if you accept these missional assumptions before moving forward.*]

Now that we have the missional assumptions to guide our process, let's look at two examples of missional questions from two exceptional permission-giving churches. These questions guide the church's leaders as they make decisions, so they know how and when to say *Yes*.

Woods Chapel United Methodist Church's Three Questions

1. Does it align with the mission?

2. Who will do it?

3. How will it be funded?

Must be grounded in prayer, discernment, and calling. (75–78)

First United Methodist Church of Sedalia's Three Questions

1. Have you prayed about it?

2. Do you believe it is God's will for us at this time? (Timing is important: do we have the right resources for sustainability, the right alignment with the priorities of the church for this ministry at this time?)

3. Will it bring glory to Jesus Christ? (80)

Group Discussion

Discuss the questions from both churches. Do they resonate with us? Is there anything missing? When our instinct is to say *No*, what are other questions we can ask to help with problem solving and offer encouragement? What questions do we want to adopt as our guiding framework for ministry?

Using the Questions

[5 minutes]

Now that we have our missional questions, turn back to the *No* example you wrote down at the end of session 1. In groups of two to three revisit one or two of the *No* scenarios and replay it with our new mission questions.

How does the new framework change the conversation?

After a few minutes we will talk as a group about how these scenarios have changed with our increasingly permission-giving atmosphere.

Closing

[5 minutes]

After these three sessions, I hope you are encouraged. We are building something exciting here. "A culture of *Yes* expects people to have ideas, gifts, and callings. It amplifies what works and encourages the passions and callings that already exist but what may remain unseen or hidden from view" (95). We are building a culture fully saying *Yes* to Jesus Christ.

At the beginning, we heard Jesus's promise that the Holy Spirit will always be with us as guide and teacher. We have started learning about and started becoming permission-giving leaders and a permission-giving church. As we close this study (or retreat) our work is not done, but we can be confident of the one we follow into the world. He says to us, "Peace I leave with you. My peace I give you. I give to you not as the world gives. Don't be troubled or afraid" (John 14:27).

Say *Yes* with peace and confidence knowing that God goes with us into the future.

As you leave, I invite you to come forward to receive an anointing with oil.

[*As they leave, anoint the participants with oil, symbolizing the Holy Spirit's anointing of their leadership and their sharing of the good news of Jesus Christ. If you feel uncomfortable with this role, invite a pastor or another leader in the church to help. Dip your finger in the oil and make the sign of the cross on the participant's forehead, and offer the following blessing.*]

You are sealed by the Holy Spirit for leadership and unleashed by the power of *Yes* in Jesus Christ.

Leave in peace and with the Spirit's power we will continue to say, *Yes*, Jesus, *Yes*! Let us say it together, *Yes*, Jesus, *Yes*!

[*Remind the participants to use their devotion guide and announce any plans you have for accountability or for sharing insights from these devotions. Also announce any next steps for implementation or action.*]

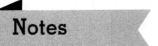

Notes

Use these pages to take notes, write out your thoughts, or sketch ideas.

Seven-Segment Devotional

Permission-Giving Leader Devotion Guide

An Introduction

During the uncover, unlock, unleash leader study, we scratched the surface of what it means to create a culture of *Yes*. This devotional guide is offered as a tool to deepen your relationship with the one who first gave you the ability to truly say *Yes*. Through the power of our creator God, our savior Jesus Christ, and our advocate the Holy Spirit, we can continue to grow into permission-giving leaders: leaders who are full of trust and hope; leaders who answer the call to love our neighbors and to go make disciples of Jesus Christ; leaders who encourage others to use their gifts and talents for the glory of God.

This devotion is designed to help unlock some of the obstacles holding you back from being an unleashed leader. Thankfully, God offers you multiple means of grace to unleash you for ministry in the world. Each session starts by naming a "lock" that may be holding you back from the fullness of leadership in Jesus Christ. Then we offer an "invitation to unlock" through the ultimate source in scripture and with insights found in Robert Schnase's book, *Just Say Yes! Unleashing People for Ministry*. Finally we offer "keys to unlock" including prayer, fasting, holy conferencing, and ideas for serving others. These keys are grace-filled opportunities to increasingly open up as a permission-giving leader. You can use this devotion for seven weeks, focusing on one session per week, or for an intense period of seven days. If you use this as a weekly devotion, here are some suggestions: reread the scripture daily and write about your insights in this book or a separate journal, spread the keys to unlock suggestions throughout the week, spend a day pondering and praying over the daily question, use the additional keys to unlock offered below, and make a plan to meet weekly with another team member to share your insights. By the end of this time of devotion, may you feel closer to God and understand more about yourself as a permission-giving leader.

Helpful Suggestions for Preparing for Your Time of Devotion

- Schedule time so you are not rushed.

- Find a quiet place without distractions.

- Have access to the Internet and/or CD player for some recommended activities.

- Have a Bible and a journal.

- Use the *Just Say Yes! Unleashing People for Ministry* book by Robert Schnase.

- Have cards to write personal notes.

- Have a white Christ candle.

Additional Keys to Unlock

If you have access to the Internet the Living Prayer Center (a ministry of The Upper Room) may be helpful (http://prayer-center.upperroom.org). This resource includes a variety of prayer methods and articles on prayer, along with help for discerning your spiritual type.

Distraction

Invitation to Unlock

God's Son, Jesus Christ, is the one who was preached among you by us—through me, Silvanus, and Timothy—he wasn't yes and no. In him it is always yes. All of God's promises have their yes in him. That is why we say Amen through him to the glory of God. God is the one who establishes us with you in Christ and who anointed us. God also sealed us and gave the Spirit as a down payment in our hearts. (2 Cor 1:19-22)

The Apostle Paul has a clarity of purpose and mission. He said *Yes* to Jesus and knows through Jesus all God's promises are *Yes*. This informs every decision he makes and gives him focus. His *Yes* gives him peace and grace to walk into the future. No matter what he faces—prison, illness, or persecution—the love of God keeps him clear about sharing this amazing gift with others.

A constant challenge for leaders is keeping everything in our lives focused on the mission and ministry of Jesus Christ. The world is moving so quickly and so many things compete for our attention. In this scripture, the Apostle Paul could easily be distracted from his purposes by the demands of life. He is forced to change his travel plans, and people begin to doubt him. They question if his words and actions line up with his ministry. He overcomes this questioning by reminding the people of Corinth that God's promises remain constant. The love and grace he continually offers the people comes from the one who is always faithful. As a leader, Paul faces everything with a clear knowledge of God's promises and focuses on his call to share the good news of Jesus Christ with others. His focus gives him clarity of purpose and helps him lead faithfully. No matter what the obstacle, he continually says *Yes* to Jesus!

Devotion Question

How are you keeping your focus on the purposes of Jesus Christ?

Keys to Unlock

These keys to unlock are to bless and enhance your devotion. They can be used immediately following the prayer or throughout daily life. They are offered as hopeful steps to help you become an increasingly permission-giving follower of Jesus Christ.

- Write down all the ways Jesus has said *Yes* in your life. What are God's promises to you? What are the "down payments" God has made on your heart (2 Cor 1:22)? Make this list a prayer of thanksgiving and end it with "through Jesus we give you all the glory God. Amen."

_____

_____

_____

- At the end of the uncover, unlock, unleash leader study, you were anointed with oil. Reread the scripture above. Do you have the same sense Paul has of being anointed and commissioned for a special mission? What is your unique mission from God?

_____

_____

_____

- When you start to pray, make note of all the distractions in your environment and in your mind. Make a plan to focus back on your time of prayer. Just as the Apostle Paul had plenty of distractions, our world continually tries to draw us away from the one who creates, saves, and sustains us. Here are some suggestions for focusing: Take time to write down all the things pulling your focus, and lift them specifically to God for guidance and blessing. Then take a moment to visualize the light of Christ settling on the place where you were sealed with oil during the study. Remember God has anointed you for leadership and lights your path.

Prayer

Attentive God, thank you for participating in my life. Saying *Yes* to you each day, I will seek to avoid the distractions of this world and remain focused on bringing your love to people. Give me clarity in the midst of busyness and noise and the ability to lead faithfully. In the name of Jesus Christ. Amen.

Apathy

Invitation to Unlock

You know I held back nothing that would be helpful so that I could proclaim to you and teach you both publicly and privately in your homes. You know I have testified to both Jews and Greeks that they must change their hearts and lives as they turn to God and have faith in our Lord Jesus. Now, compelled by the Spirit, I'm going to Jerusalem. I don't know what will happen to me there. What I do know is that the Holy Spirit testifies to me from city to city that prisons and troubles await me. But nothing, not even my life, is more important than my completing my mission. This is nothing other than the ministry I received from the Lord Jesus: to testify about the good news of God's grace. (Acts 20:20-24)

Everything about the Apostle Paul's life changed once he meets and commits to following Jesus Christ. His language exudes a passion and devotion to God. He even considers his life nothing but a tool for offering the grace of God for others. Paul says no matter what obstacles he faces, he is willing to do it for the cause of Jesus Christ. The message is worthy of any sacrifice. This is what Schnase refers to as imperative. "*Imperative* refers to drive, passion, momentum, excitement, and desire that motivates ministry" (46). He goes on to share how

[Leaders and] congregations with a sense of imperative believe that the work of Christ is absolutely necessary, vital to life and rebirth, and that inviting people into the spiritual life is something that must be done. They operate under the mandates of Christ, the imperatives that lace the teachings of Jesus: "Go.... Teach.... Heal.... Welcome.... Give.... Serve.... Pray.... Do.... Love.... Follow." (47)

Devotion Question

Do you have imperative drive for the mission and purposes of Christ?

Keys to Unlock

These keys to unlock are to bless and enhance your devotion. They can be used immediately following the prayer or throughout daily life. They are offered as hopeful steps to help you become an increasingly permission-giving follower of Jesus Christ.

- Take a few minutes to reread pages 45–49 in *Just Say Yes!* under the heading, "A Sense of Imperative." Thinking about the asthma example in this section, imagine the feeling: "You can breathe again, all fear is gone, and there's new energy and vitality" (47). With this sense, practice the following breath prayer in a place of quiet and comfort. First, take a deep breath in and then hold it. Pay attention to your body and hold it until you are desperate for breath. Then repeatedly, passionately breathe in the name of God, and then breathe out your plea for help. For example, breathe in saying, "creator God" and breathe out saying "breathe life in me." Here are phrases to help you begin: "Creator God, breathe life in me." "Lord Jesus, save me." "Holy Spirit, make me yours."

- Write down your passions. How are you using them for the mission and purposes of Jesus Christ?

_____

_____

_____

- Remember a story of how Jesus grabbed hold of your life and find a way to share it with someone this week. It can be a note of encouragement, a call, or a time to share coffee.

Prayer

Active God, help me create imperative in my life and ministry. Remind me what it means to passionately follow you and long to share your good news with others. Instill in me overflowing love and hope that will positively impact your people. In the name of Jesus Christ. Amen.

Lock #3

Fear

I am the LORD your God, / who grasps your strong hand, / who says to you, / Don't fear; I will help you. (Isa 41:13)

You didn't receive a spirit of slavery to lead you back again into fear, but you received a Spirit that shows you are adopted as his children. With this Spirit, we cry, "Abba, Father." (Rom 8:15)

God didn't give us a spirit that is timid but one that is powerful, loving, and self-controlled. (2 Tim 1:7)

Throughout scripture, in both Old and New Testaments, God calls us from fear toward trust. Permission-giving leaders are grounded in trust and hope. This allows them to be creative and encouraging to others. Out of this encouragement, innovation and dreaming happens and things change. Change can bring us back to fear if we are not careful and intentional to grow in faith. Schnase's book asks an important question about why we struggle with change.

> Why do people resist change and reject new ideas even when they know that the old habits, attitudes, and systems are holding them back from doing greater good? [Leadership author] Ronald Heifetz says that people do not fear change; they fear loss. People fear the grief that comes with losing what has been familiar, reliable, and known; habits, values, and attitudes—even those that have been barriers to progress and unhelpful for the mission—are part of one's identity, and changing them challenges how we define ourselves" (7–8).

Fear is powerful, but the love and grace of Jesus Christ can overcome the greatest of fear. Putting our trust in Jesus Christ is the key to being leaders who continually are willing to risk for the glory of God's kingdom.

Devotion Question

How do you overcome fear of change and loss?

Keys to Unlock

These keys to unlock are to bless and enhance your devotion. They can be used immediately following the prayer or throughout daily life. They are offered as hopeful steps to help you become an increasingly permission-giving follower of Jesus Christ.

- Pick one of the scripture passages from above to use in a *lectio divina* prayer exercise. You will read the text three times. During the first reading, pay attention to what word or phrase takes your focus. Write down this word or phrase. During the second reading, focus on what images and thoughts this word or phrase brings to mind. Take some time to draw an image from your thoughts, journal, or go for a walk praying for God to speak to you. During the third reading, read it out loud and hear any challenge God may be giving you through the text. What do you need to do or say to faithfully live into this message from God's word? Leave this time of prayer with comfort and confidence in your connection with the living God.

- Think of a time when you were afraid. How did God help you overcome the fear? When change has happened in church, what losses were the hardest for you to accept? Why?

44

_____

_____

_____

- Take a few moments to rest in the constancy of God's love and grace for you. Fear can be overcome with the assurance of God's forever faithfulness. Listen to or play a song that helps you feel the faithfulness of God. If you have access to the Internet, a possible song is "One Thing Remains" by Bethel Music, performed by Jesus Culture.

Prayer

Steadfast God, bring me into your presence in moments of fear. May I trust you more faithfully in moments of change and loss. Help me to see your creative work in this world and be excited about the possibilities you place in my path. With certainty in you, allow me to lead others well in moments of change. In the name of Jesus Christ. Amen.

Lock # 4

Negativity

Invitation to Unlock

Don't let any foul words come out of your mouth. Only say what is helpful when it is needed for building up the community so that it benefits those who hear what you say. (Eph 4:29)

These words are crucial to hear and repeat today. Words hold great power to tear down or to inspire. Think of the dramatic difference between a time when someone hurt you with words and a time when someone used words to lift you up. When we speak negative words, we may be discouraging or stopping the passions and gifts of others in our midst.

The *No* person looks for problems, and then focuses exclusively on how to fix them.... "I serve a dysfunctional church," a pastor says. "I could never get my people to do that." [Or] "That would never work here," a layperson laments. "Our church doesn't have enough people or money." The repetition and reinforcement of these negative perceptions create a self-fulfilling prophecy. Leaders who focus exclusively on what's broken...and what can't happen foster an environment that makes change impossible. (95)

Devotion Question

Author Robert Schnase challenges us to ask, "What if we believed that we have exactly enough people and resources to fulfill the ministry God is calling us to today?" (95).

Keys to Unlock

These keys to unlock are to bless and enhance your devotion. They can be used immediately following the prayer or throughout daily life. They are offered as hopeful steps to help you become an increasingly permission-giving follower of Jesus Christ.

- Recall from the *Just Say Yes!* study the video, "Unleashing Systems: Creating a Culture Shift." (If you have access to the DVD or streamed video clip, you might take a look at it again.) In this video, Rev. Jim Downing says there are two common "rails" churches operate on: "we've always done it this way" (stuck in the past) and "we've never done it that way before" (fear of failure). In his ministry context, they created a mission jar and anytime anyone started to say anything negative like these two phrases they paid one dollar for missions. Create a jar for yourself and place one dollar in for missions any time negative words come from your mouth. Positivity and hope will become a habit.

_____

_____

_____

- What negativity do you carry in your heart about the ministries or people in your congregation? It is nearly impossible to stay negative when you come face to face with the light of Christ. Get a white candle and find a quiet and preferably dark space to light the candle. Before you turn out the room light, light the candle and read Matthew 5:14-16: "You are the light of the world. A city on top of a hill can't be hidden. Neither do people light a lamp and put it under a basket. Instead, they put it on top of a lampstand, and it shines on all who are in the house. In the same way, let your light shine before people, so they can see the good things you do and praise your Father who is in heaven." Believe deep in your heart this is the light of Christ burning away any negativity you carry. Christ's light is the hope, joy, and love you will carry into the world with you. Stay in an attitude of meditation as long as you feel connected to the light of Christ.

_____

_____

_____

- Take a few moments to read the "instead of" questions on pages 65–66 of *Just Say Yes!* Which strike you as the most challenging and the most empowering?

_____

_____

_____

Prayer

Inspiring God, may I rely on your hope in moments of difficulty and negativity. Help me to speak words that build up rather than tear down people. Give me your joy each day so I can offer hope to people who are worried or afraid in this world. In the name of Jesus Christ. Amen.

Lock # 5

Selfishness

Therefore, if there is any encouragement in Christ, any comfort in love, any sharing in the Spirit, any sympathy, complete my joy by thinking the same way, having the same love, being united, and agreeing with each other. Don't do anything for selfish purposes, but with humility think of others as better than yourselves. Instead of each person watching out for their own good, watch out for what is better for others. (Phil 2:1-4)

When we make ourselves the focus of our decision-making, we push Christ from the center of our lives. The scripture talks of the difference between selfish purposes and the encouraging, loving, joyful purposes of Christ. Schnase says this about our struggles with selfishness, "We align the ministries with our preferences rather than discerning what aligns with Christ's work. We become protective, defensive, controlling, and territorial. We say *No*" (9). When we make it all about us, we ask "'What's in it for me?'... 'How does this affect me? Will I benefit from it?' And most importantly, 'What will I have to do? What will it cost me?'"(10)

When we ask questions like these, how is the love of God evident in our lives and leadership? Do our actions show we are "watch[ing] out for what is better for others"?

Devotion Question

How are you sharing your time, resources, gifts, and passions to show your love of God and neighbor?

Keys to Unlock

These keys to unlock are to bless and enhance your devotion. They can be used immediately following the prayer or throughout daily life. They are offered as hopeful steps to help you become an increasingly permission-giving follower of Jesus Christ.

- Serving others is the best way to counter selfishness. Create a graph matrix like the one described in *Just Say Yes!* (see 57–59) and the example below. Make the left side of the graph needs you see in the world. Along the bottom write your personal interests, gifts, passions, and talents. Find the intersection. Are there others doing this type of ministry you can join or should you start a prayer of discernment around using your gifts? If you are uncertain about the gifts God has given you, please take some time to do a spiritual gifts inventory. Try this one from the United Methodist tradition or use one from your tradition: http://www.umc .org/what-we-believe/spiritual-gifts-online-assessment.

Needs I See in the World That Break My Heart	Illiteracy in Children	I could offer my skills to write about the needs. Possibly educate people at church and beyond.	I could donate books to after school Christian reading/tutoring ministries.	I could volunteer to read with kids at an after school reading ministry.
	Kids in Foster Care	I could offer my skills to write about the needs. Possibly educate people at church and beyond.	I could donate items to ministries that help kids in transition.	I could train to do respite care for foster care families.
		Writing	Generosity	Good with Children
		My Passion, Gifts, and Talents		

- This week, find a way to intentionally show the love of Jesus Christ to others through service. This is not about us—this is about giving thanks for what God has done for us. By serving others, we will be living "the pattern of gracious love" we read above.

- Humility Prayer—If you typically pray sitting up, consider praying on your knees. If you normally pray on your knees, consider praying prostrate (lay with your face down). Increase your physical expression of humility and offer a prayer such as the Wesley Covenant prayer (contemporary version) from the Methodist tradition or one of your own.

Prayer

Generous God, thank you for all you give to me daily. All that I am and all that I have are gifts from you. I long to model my life after your example of humility through Jesus Christ. The life, death and resurrection of Jesus are testaments to how willing you are to give extravagantly to your people. Help me focus on loving and serving others in my decision-making and in our church ministries. In the name of Jesus Christ. Amen.

Lock #6

Control

Invitation to Unlock

As Jesus walked alongside the Galilee Sea, he saw two brothers, Simon, who is called Peter, and Andrew, throwing fishing nets into the sea, because they were fishermen. "Come, follow me," he said, "and I'll show you how to fish for people." Right away, they left their nets and followed him. (Matt 4:18-20)

When we are called to follow Jesus, we do not know where this may lead us. This takes control out of our hands. Following Jesus means first remembering you are a follower and then a leader. This takes faith in the one you follow. "The essence of faith is captured in the words that describe Abraham's obedience to God's call, 'He went out without knowing where he was going' (Heb 11:8)" (5).

It is easy to feel a need to hold the reigns tight when you are a leader. Yet a need for control makes it nearly impossible to truly *follow Jesus*. When we want to constantly have the final say in decision making, believe it has to be done by us, and have to know everything, we often say *No*. Recognizing God's call and gifting of other people means there will be ministries happening beyond one person's control. Permission-giving leaders know relinquishing control can be messy but also realize saying *Yes* to Jesus is worth it.

"Unleashing people for ministry sets a church on an unpredictable path. It multiplies ministry. It interrupts the business as usual. *Yes* unleashes the wild, raw nature of God" (90).

The disciples threw down their nets, their way of life, to follow Jesus into an uncertain future. That act of faith allowed them to witness the extraordinary good news of the life, death, and resurrection of Jesus Christ. Their willingness to follow helped the good news reach us today.

Devotion Question

What will your leadership legacy be? Will you be the one who "killed ideas, closed down initiatives, curtailed the ministries of energetic and passionate people"? Or, will you "be the person God works through rather than the person God has to work around"? (13).

Keys to Unlock

These keys to unlock are to bless and enhance your devotion. They can be used immediately following the prayer or throughout daily life. They are offered as hopeful steps to help you become an increasingly permission-giving follower of Jesus Christ.

- Consider trying a Wesley fast, which comes from the Methodist tradition. Feel free to use another form of fasting if Methodism is not your tradition. "The Wesley Fast, traditionally observed, begins with dinner on Thursday evening and continues until tea time on Friday. Time and energy that would have been consumed in eating is offered for deeper prayer, meditation and works of charity and compassion. When, for health reasons such a fast is not advisable, persons are encouraged to adjust the fast to their personal needs. Please remember to drink plenty of juice and water" (http://www.umc.org/who-we-are/call-to-prayer -and-fasting). The time you spend fasting can be used to focus on faith and your dependence on God. It can help reorient your leadership from control to following and believing God is gifting others with ideas for ministries. If a medical reason makes a food fast unsafe, please consider refraining from other activities such as social media, talking, and so on.

- Find a person in the congregation you trust to talk with about your leadership style. Have them help you discern times when they have witnessed you try to hold onto control. Pray with them and ask them to hold you accountable for leading with obedience to Christ's mandates and not your own.

- In addition to meeting with others to talk about leadership, you can form a covenant or accountability group. Each meeting you could share joys and concerns, where you have seen God moving in your life, and your current struggles related to faithfulness.

Prayer

Empowering God, you have given me amazing opportunities to lead in your name. Remind me not to seek to control or micromanage ministry. I never want to be in the way of your work in the world. Remind me daily that I follow you and you are worthy of all my faith. Out of this faith, help me partner with you to unleash people for ministry. In the name of Jesus Christ. Amen.

Discouragement

Invitation to Unlock

Let's hold on to the confession of our hope without wavering, because the one who made the promises is reliable. And let us consider each other carefully for the purpose of sparking love and good deeds. Don't stop meeting together with other believers, which some people have gotten into the habit of doing. Instead, encourage each other, especially as you see the day drawing near. (Heb 10:23-25)

A discouraged congregation will hear more *Nos* than *Yeses*. The people will be less likely to dream and more likely to focus on themselves. They will show less love, do less service, and be more afraid of change. Yet this kind of culture can change with hope. Hebrews tells us we can have hope because God's promises are reliable. We are called to "spark love and good deeds" in each other as followers of Jesus Christ. Permission-giving leaders have hope and they encourage others!

> *Encouragement* literally means "to fill with courage and strength of purpose, to hearten, to give heart." Encouragement refers to the action of giving someone support, confidence, and hope.... to inspire and motivatee....[It] emboldens rather than restrains, empowers rather than limits, stimulates people to move forward rather than to retreat....Real encouragement means helping people say *Yes* to God." (112–13)

Encouragement not only lifts up the individual but it builds up the entire community of faith.

Devotion Question

How do we stop discouraging and become encouragers?

55

Keys to Unlock

These keys to unlock are to bless and enhance your devotion. They can be used immediately following the prayer or throughout daily life. They are offered as hopeful steps to help you become an increasingly permission-giving follower of Jesus Christ.

- Spend some focused time in prayer for others in your congregation. Before you pray the following prayer, think of specific people in the congregation you want to lift to God. Who needs encouragement for tough life situations, needs encouragement to answer a call to ministry, and longs for connection and purpose? *Encouraging and empowering God, your word tells us we are part of your son's body. Help us remember, "The whole body grows from him, as it is joined and held together by all the supporting ligaments. The body makes itself grow in that it builds itself up with love as each one does its part" (Eph 4:16). We need your help to grow. We need your help to properly use the gifts you have given each of us. We need your help to encourage each other in love. Please hear this urgent plea to encourage _____, who is in desperate need of hope. Please hear my hopeful plea for you to help _____, to answer their call to ministry. Please hear my grateful plea to empower _____, who needs a place to connect, a purpose, and longs to serve. I praise you God for this opportunity to lift my fellow brothers and sisters to you with confidence my prayers will be heard. May your will be done in this place. Amen.*

- Permission-giving leaders spend time with others. They help people at all stages of faith to listen to God, "to follow their callings, explore ideas they are curious about, and experiment with new approaches" (99). Who is the first person that comes to mind when you think of someone at church who needs encouragement to follow his or her God-given dreams? Consider inviting him or her to coffee or writing him or her a note of encouragement. Here are some thoughts on encouraging others:
    - o Pray with them and for them.
    - o Help them connect with others who might have similar passions, invite them to do a spiritual gifts inventory, and ask questions to help them dream.

o Encourage them to do a graph like the one mentioned in lock #5 of this devotional guide if they want help finding their purpose.

Prayer

Encouraging God, lift me up in moments I become discouraged in ministry. Allow my leadership to be centered on loving you and my neighbors. Give me courage, strength of purpose, and heart so I can share this with others. Inspire and motivate me to remain a person of *Yes*, one who helps others say *Yes* to you. In the name of Jesus Christ. Amen.

Appendix

Next Steps

These options can be used for subsequent work for an expanded weekend retreat setting or at a follow-up meeting for the team after completing the devotion. Use these next steps to keep unleashing your church for ministry:

1. If you are the pastor, plan to do the *Just Say Yes! Sermon and Worship Series*. The sermon outlines and worship helps are available for free download online at RobertSchnase.com and Cokesbury.com. Obtain copies of the companion four-week devotional for your congregants, and urge them to use it as a weekly sermon study and devotional guide during the series. If you are not the pastor, encourage the pastor to do this, and offer to help!

2. Encourage the small group study participants to share their insights from working through the seven-segment devotional. You may want to set up a private Facebook group for sharing or plan a time to share the ways God is working in each of the leaders.

3. Look at the list of *Nos* we have said in the past year, and see if there are people we need to invite back into dreaming. If there are specific *Nos* to be revisited, it is helpful to assign a representative to revisit the people with dreams for ministry.

4. Ask a study participant who has really thrived in this study to write an article for the community newsletter, share his or her testimony in worship, or lead an informational meeting for the congregation.

5. Use the information in chapter 3 of *Just Say Yes!* to take a look at ways your church may be saying *No* to ideas and people. Often we say *No* without even realizing it, and this chapter helps identify these moments and adjust accordingly.

6. Host a video watch party and brainstorming session with leaders and congregants. Invite congregants to do some of the activities from the small group study for leaders.

7. What other ideas for next steps do you have?

Descriptions of *Just Say Yes!* Video Clips

Just Say Yes! Introductory Video

Robert Schnase shares how *Just Say Yes! Unleashing People for Ministry* can offer hope for those people whose passion has been simmering for years.

Unlocking the Power of Yes: Becoming More Permission Giving

Rev. Jennifer Weekes-Klein, senior pastor of Country Club United Methodist Church in Kansas City, shares the necessary personal and spiritual work that needs to be done in order to unlock the power of *Yes* in your life.

Unleashing Systems: Creating a Culture Shift

Rev. Jim Downing, senior pastor of First United Methodist Church of Sedalia, shares how leaders can work to create a cultural shift from a *No* culture to a permission-giving culture.

Failure-Tolerant Leadership

Rev. Tina Harris, pastor of Grand Avenue Temple in Kansas City, reminds leaders how, sometimes, failures can be the best example of following Jesus.

Permission-Giving Leadership: When *No* Is the Right Answer

Rev. Matt Miofsky, senior pastor of The Gathering in St. Louis, stresses that ideas that do not align with mission, priorities, and the spirit of the church are legitimate reasons to say *No*.

Legacy: Clayton UMC and The Gathering

Unlike many "legacy church" stories, Clayton United Methodist Church was not in imminent danger of closing. Yet they wanted their legacy to be one of life not death. Their decision to close years before circumstances demanded they do so allowed them to gift The Gathering approximately $250,000, a building, and a desire to see something new take root.

A New Way of Being: Sturgeon UMC

The story of Sturgeon United Methodist Church was all too common: too small, too old, too tired. Under the unifying direction of Rev. Mike Will, they joined forces with the four other local churches and forged a new way of being church to their broader community.

Hope in the Baking: Bridge Bread

Lafayette Park United Methodist Church is an urban local church in one of the oldest parts of St. Louis. Through prayer and discernment, a small group of disciples began exploring the ministry and business of social enterprise, and bridge bread was born.

Kuomba Pamoja (Worship Together): Central UMC

Central United Methodist Church, a largely Anglo, affluent congregation, has approximately fifty to sixty African worshippers thanks to the invitational nature of Mama Riziki. Slowly, through the hard work of building relationship, Central United Methodist Church is beginning to *kuomba pamoja* or "worship together."

Warm Start—Beginning to Know Jesus: Asbury UMC

The people of Asbury United Methodist church in the historic greater neighborhood of north St. Louis are serving the children of their neighborhood one juice box at a time.

CPSIA information can be obtained
at www.ICGtesting.com
Printed in the USA
LVOW04s0737290316

481145LV00002B/2/P

9 781501 825262